The Elements of Style

THE ELEMENTS OF STYLE

by

WILLIAM STRUNK, JR.

*With Revisions, an Introduction, and
a New Chapter on Writing*

by E. B. WHITE

The Macmillan Company

MACMILLAN PAPERBACKS EDITION 1962

Library of Congress catalog card number: 59-9950

THE MACMILLAN COMPANY
866 THIRD AVENUE, NEW YORK, NEW YORK 10022
Collier-Macmillan Canada, Ltd., Toronto, Ontario
Twenty-Second Printing, 1970

The Introduction originally appeared, in slightly different form, in *The New Yorker,* and was copyrighted in 1957 by The New Yorker Magazine, Inc.

The Elements of Style, Revised Edition, by William Strunk, Jr., and Edward A. Tenney, Copyright 1935 by Oliver Strunk.

Printed in the United States of America

A Note on This Book

In the summer of 1957, I wrote a piece for *The New Yorker* about a textbook I had used when I was a student at Cornell. The book dealt with usage and style; the author was William Strunk, Jr., who had been my friend and teacher. When this piece of mine appeared in print, the editors of The Macmillan Company got hold of the textbook and arranged to reissue it, using my article as an introduction. They asked me to make revisions in the text and write a chapter on style, and I have done both things.

Professor Strunk was a positive man. His book contained rules of grammar phrased as direct orders. In the main I have not attempted to soften his commands, or modify his pronouncements, or delete the special objects of his scorn. I have tried, instead, to preserve the flavor of his discontent, while slightly enlarging the scope of the discussion. I did omit one intricate rule of composition—one that I suspected the author might have cut had he been alive today. In its place appears Rule 8, a substitution I thought proper and for which the reader must not hold Professor Strunk responsible. Here and there in the book, minor alterations have been made; a few outdated references have been dropped, a few fresh examples added. Mr. Strunk had once done some revising of his text, for subsequent editions; some of his revisions are retained here, others are not.

The Elements of Style, as originally conceived, was not an attempt to survey the whole field. In an introduction to his first edition, the author stated that he intended merely to give in brief space the principal requirements of plain

English style. He proposed, he said, to concentrate on fundamentals: the rules of usage and principles of composition most commonly violated. Essentially, his statement of purpose and scope remains valid for this new edition.

The final chapter of the original book was about spelling. That chapter has been discarded. In its place is the one I have contributed, Chapter V, called "An Approach to Style." Professor Strunk, it must be clearly understood, had no part in this escapade, and I have no way of knowing whether he would approve. These are strictly my own prejudices, my notions of error, my articles of faith. The chapter is addressed particularly to those who feel that English prose composition is not only a necessary skill but a sensible pursuit as well—a way to spend one's days. I think Professor Strunk would not object to that.

E. B. White

Introduction

A small book arrived in my mail not long ago, a gift from a friend in Ithaca. It is *The Elements of Style,* by the late William Strunk, Jr., and it was known on the Cornell campus in my day as "the little book," with the stress on the word "little." I must have once owned a copy, for I took English 8 under Professor Strunk in 1919 and the book was required reading, but my copy presumably failed to survive an early purge. I had not laid eyes on it in thirty-eight years, and I was delighted to study it again and rediscover its rich deposits of gold.

The Elements of Style was Will Strunk's *parvum opus,* his attempt to cut the vast tangle of English rhetoric down to size and write its rules and principles on the head of a pin. Will himself hung the title "little" on the book: he referred to it sardonically and with secret pride as "the *little* book," always giving the word "little" a special twist, as though he were putting a spin on a ball. The title page reveals that the book was privately printed (Ithaca, N.Y.) and that it was copyrighted in 1918 by the author. It is a forty-three-page summation of the case for cleanliness, accuracy, and brevity in the use of English. Its vigor is unimpaired, and for sheer pith I think it probably sets a record that is not likely to be broken. The Cornell University Library has one copy. It had two, but my friend pried one loose and mailed it to me.

The book consists of a short introduction, eight rules of usage, ten principles of composition, a few matters of form, a list of words and expressions commonly misused, a list of words commonly misspelled. That's all there is. The rules and principles are in the form of direct commands, Sergeant Strunk snapping orders to his platoon. "Do not join independent clauses by a comma." (Rule 5.) "Do not break sentences in two." (Rule 6.) "Use the active voice." (Rule 10.) "Omit needless words." (Rule 13.) "Avoid a succession of loose sentences." (Rule 14.) "In summaries, keep to one tense." (Rule 17.) Each rule or principle is followed by a short hortatory essay, and the exhortation is followed by, or interlarded with, examples in parallel columns—the true vs. the false, the right vs. the wrong, the timid vs. the bold, the ragged vs. the trim. From every line there peers out at me the puckish face of my professor, his short hair parted neatly in the middle and combed down over his forehead, his eyes blinking incessantly behind steel-rimmed spectacles as though he had just emerged into strong light, his lips nibbling each other like nervous horses, his smile shuttling to and fro in a carefully edged mustache.

"Omit needless words!" cries the author on page 17, and into that imperative Will Strunk really put his heart and soul. In the days when I was sitting in his class, he omitted so many needless words, and omitted them so forcibly and with such eagerness and obvious relish, that he often seemed in the position of having short-changed himself, a man left with nothing more to say yet with time to fill, a radio prophet who had outdistanced the clock. Will Strunk got out of this predicament by a simple trick: he uttered every sentence three times. When he delivered his oration on brevity to the class, he leaned forward over his desk, grasped his coat lapels in his hands, and in a husky, conspiratorial voice said, "Rule Thirteen. Omit needless words! Omit needless words! Omit needless words!"

He was a memorable man, friendly and funny. Under the remembered sting of his kindly lash, I have been trying to omit needless words since 1919, and although there are still many words that cry for omission and the huge task will never be accomplished, it is exciting to me to reread the masterly Strunkian elaboration of this noble theme. It goes:

Vigorous writing is concise. A sentence should contain no unnecessary words, a paragraph no unnecessary sentences, for the same reason that a drawing should have no unnecessary lines and a machine no unnecessary parts. This requires not that the writer make all his sentences short, or that he avoid all detail and treat his subjects only in outline, but that every word tell.

There you have a short, valuable essay on the nature and beauty of brevity—sixty-three words that could change the world. Having recovered from his adventure in prolixity (sixty-three words were a lot of words in the tight world of William Strunk, Jr.), the Professor proceeds to give a few quick lessons in pruning. The student learns to cut the deadwood from "This is a subject which . . . ," reducing it to "This subject . . . ," a gain of three words. He learns to trim ". . . used for fuel purposes" down to "used for fuel." He learns that he is being a chatterbox when he says "The question as to whether" and that he should just say "Whether"—a gain of four words out of a possible five.

The Professor devotes a special paragraph to the vile expression "the fact that," a phrase that causes him to quiver with revulsion. The expression, he says, should be "revised out of every sentence in which it occurs." But a shadow of gloom seems to hang over the page, and you feel that he knows how hopeless his cause is. I suppose I have written "the fact that" a thousand times in the heat of composition, revised it out maybe five hundred times in the cool aftermath. To be batting only .500 this late in the season, to fail half the time to connect with this fat pitch, saddens me, for it seems a betrayal of the man who showed me how to swing at it and made the swinging seem worth while.

I treasure The Elements of Style for its sharp advice, but I treasure it even more for the audacity and self-confidence of its author. Will knew where he stood. He was so sure of where he stood, and made his position so clear and so plausible, that his peculiar stance has continued to invigorate me—and, I am sure, thousands of other ex-students—during the years that have intervened since our first encounter. He had a number of likes and dislikes that were almost as whimsical as the choice of a necktie, yet he made them seem utterly convincing. He disliked the word "forceful" and advised us to use "forcible" instead. He felt that the word "clever" was greatly overused; "it is best restricted to ingenuity displayed in small matters." He despised the expression "student body," which he termed gruesome, and made a special trip downtown to the *Alumni News* office one day to protest the expression and suggest that "studentry" be substituted, a coinage of his own which he felt was similar to "citizenry." I am told that the *News* editor was so charmed by the visit, if not by the word, that he ordered the student body buried, never to rise again. "Studentry" has taken its place. It's not much of an improvement, but it does sound less cadaverous, and it made Will Strunk quite happy.

A few weeks ago I noticed a headline in the *Times* about Bonnie Prince Charlie: "CHARLES' TONSILS OUT." Immediately Rule 1 leapt to mind.

1. Form the possessive singular of nouns by adding 's. Follow this rule whatever the final consonant. Thus write,

Charles's friend
Burns's poems
the witch's malice

Clearly, Will Strunk had foreseen, as far back as 1918, the dangerous tonsillectomy of a prince, in which the surgeon removes the tonsils and the *Times* copy desk removes the final "s." He started his book with it. I commend Rule 1 to the *Times* and I trust that Charles's throat, not Charles' throat, is mended.

Style rules of this sort are, of course, somewhat a matter of individual preference, and even the established rules of grammar are open to challenge. Professor Strunk, although one of the most inflexible and choosy of men, was quick to acknowledge the fallacy of inflexibility and the danger of doctrine.

"It is an old observation," he wrote, "that the best writers sometimes disregard the rules of rhetoric. When they do so, however, the reader will usually find in the sentence some compensating merit, attained at the cost of the violation. Unless he is certain of doing as well, he will probably do best to follow the rules."

It is encouraging to see how perfectly a book, even a dusty rulebook, perpetuates and extends the spirit of a man. Will Strunk loved the clear, the brief, the bold, and his book is clear, brief, bold. Boldness is perhaps its chief distinguishing mark. On page 21, explaining one of his parallels, he says, "The left-hand version gives the impression that the writer is undecided or timid; he seems unable or afraid to choose one form of expression and hold to it." And his Rule 11 is "Make definite assertions." That was Will all over. He scorned the vague, the tame, the colorless, the irresolute. He felt it was worse to be irresolute than to be wrong. I remember a day in class when he leaned far forward in his characteristic pose—the pose of a man about to impart a secret—and croaked, "If you don't know how to pronounce a word, say it loud! If you don't know how to pronounce a word, say it loud!" This comical piece of advice struck me as sound at the time, and I still respect it. Why compound ignorance with inaudibility? Why run and hide?

All through *The Elements of Style* one finds evidences of the author's deep sympathy for the reader. Will felt that the reader was in serious trouble most of the time, a man floundering in a swamp, and that it was the duty of anyone attempting to write English to drain this swamp quickly and get his man up on dry ground, or at least throw him a rope.

"The little book" has long since passed into disuse. Will died in 1946, and he had retired from teaching several years before that. Longer, lower textbooks are in use in English classes nowadays, I daresay—books with upswept tail fins and automatic verbs. I hope some of them manage to compress as much wisdom into as small a space, manage to come to the point as quickly and illuminate it as amusingly. I think, though, that if I suddenly found myself in the, to me, unthinkable position of facing a class in English usage and style, I would simply lean far out over the desk, clutch my lapels, blink my eyes, and say, "Get the *little* book! Get the *little* book! Get the *little* book!"

Contents

The Elements of Style

I

Elementary Rules of Usage

1. Form the possessive singular of nouns by adding 's.
Follow this rule whatever the final consonant. Thus write,

> Charles's friend
> Burns's poems
> the witch's malice

Exceptions are the possessives of ancient proper names in
-es and *-is*, the possessive *Jesus'*, and such forms as *for con-
science' sake, for righteousness' sake*. But such forms as
Moses' laws, Isis' temple are commonly replaced by

> the laws of Moses
> the temple of Isis

The pronominal possessives *hers, its, theirs, yours,* and
oneself have no apostrophe.

**2. In a series of three or more terms with a single con-
junction, use a comma after each term except the last.**
Thus write,

red, white, and blue
gold, silver, or copper
He opened the letter, read it, and made a note of its contents.

This comma is often referred to as the "serial" comma.

In the names of business firms the last comma is usually omitted. Follow the usage of the individual firm.

> Brown, Shipley and Co.
> Merrill Lynch, Pierce, Fenner & Smith Incorporated

3. Enclose parenthetic expressions between commas.

The best way to see a country, unless you are pressed for time, is to travel on foot.

This rule is difficult to apply; it is frequently hard to decide whether a single word, such as *however,* or a brief phrase, is or is not parenthetic. If the interruption to the flow of the sentence is but slight, the writer may safely omit the commas. But whether the interruption be slight or considerable, he must never omit one comma and leave the other. There is no defense for such punctuation as

> Marjorie's husband, Colonel Nelson paid us a visit yesterday.

or

> My brother you will be pleased to hear, is now in perfect health.

Dates usually contain parenthetic words or figures. Punctuate as follows:

> February to July, 1956
> April 6, 1936
> Wednesday, November 13, 1929

Note that it is permissible to omit the comma in

> 6 April 1958

The last form is an excellent way to write a date; the figures are separated by a word and are, for that reason, quickly grasped.

A name or a title in direct address is parenthetic.

If, Sir, you refuse, I cannot predict what will happen.
Well, Susan, this is a fine mess you are in.

The abbreviations *etc.* and *jr.* are parenthetic and are always to be so regarded.

James Wright, Jr.
Letters, packages, etc., should go here.

Nonrestrictive relative clauses are parenthetic, as are similar clauses introduced by conjunctions indicating time or place. Commas are therefore needed. A nonrestrictive clause is one that does not serve to identify or define the antecedent noun.

The audience, which had at first been indifferent, became more and more interested.
In 1769, when Napoleon was born, Corsica had but recently been acquired by France.
Nether Stowey, where Coleridge wrote *The Rime of the Ancient Mariner,* is a few miles from Bridgewater.

In these sentences, the clauses introduced by *which,* *when,* and *where* are nonrestrictive; they do not limit or define, they merely add something. In the first example, the clause introduced by *which* does not serve to tell which of several possible audiences is meant; the reader presumably knows that already. The clause adds, parenthetically, a statement supplementing that in the main clause. Each of the three sentences is a combination of two statements that might have been made independently.

The audience was at first indifferent. Later it became more and more interested.

3

Napoleon was born in 1769. At that time Corsica had but recently been acquired by France.

Coleridge wrote *The Rime of the Ancient Mariner* at Nether Stowey. Nether Stowey is only a few miles from Bridgewater.

Restrictive clauses, by contrast, are not parenthetic and are not set off by commas. Thus,

People who live in glass houses shouldn't throw stones.

Here the clause introduced by *who* does serve to tell which people are meant; the sentence, unlike those above, cannot be split into two independent statements.

When the main clause of a sentence is preceded by, or followed by, a phrase or a dependent clause, use commas to set off these elements. This rule is similar in principle to the rule governing parenthetic expressions.

Partly by hard fighting, partly by diplomatic skill, they enlarged their dominions to the east and rose to royal rank with the possession of Sicily, exchanged afterwards for Sardinia.

4. Place a comma before a conjunction introducing an independent clause.

The early records of the city have disappeared, and the story of its first years can no longer be reconstructed.

The situation is perilous, but there is still one chance of escape.

Sentences of this type, isolated from their context, may seem to be in need of rewriting. As they make complete sense when the comma is reached, the second clause has the appearance of an afterthought. Further, *and* is the least specific of connectives. Used between independent clauses, it indicates only that a relation exists between them without defining that relation. In the example above, the relation is that of cause and result. The two sentences might be rewritten:

Because the early records of the city have disappeared, the story of its first years can no longer be reconstructed.
Although the situation is perilous, there is still one chance of escape.

Or the subordinate clauses might be replaced by phrases:

Owing to the disappearance of the early records of the city, the story of its first years can no longer be reconstructed.
In this perilous situation, there is still one chance of escape.

But a writer may err by making his sentences too uniformly compact and periodic, and an occasional loose sentence prevents the style from becoming too formal and gives the reader a certain relief. Consequently, loose sentences of the type first quoted are common in easy, unstudied writing. The danger is that there be too many of them (see Rule 14).

Two-part sentences of which the second member is introduced by *as* (in the sense of *because*), *for, or, nor,* and *while* (in the sense of *and at the same time*) likewise require a comma before the conjunction.

If a dependent clause, or an introductory phrase requiring to be set off by a comma, precedes the second independent clause, no comma is needed after the conjunction.

The situation is perilous, but if we are prepared to act promptly, there is still one chance of escape.

When the subject is the same for both clauses and is expressed only once, a comma is required if the connective is *but.* If the connective is *and,* the comma should be omitted if the relation between the two statements is close or immediate.

I have heard his arguments, but am still unconvinced.

He has had several years' experience and is thoroughly competent.

5. *Do not join independent clauses by a comma.*

If two or more clauses, grammatically complete and not joined by a conjunction, are to form a single compound sentence, the proper mark of punctuation is a semicolon.

Stevenson's romances are entertaining; they are full of exciting adventures.
It is nearly half past five; we cannot reach town before dark.

It is, of course, equally correct to write these as two sentences each, replacing the semicolons with periods.

Stevenson's romances are entertaining. They are full of exciting adventures.
It is nearly half past five. We cannot reach town before dark.

If a conjunction is inserted, the proper mark is a comma (Rule 4).

Stevenson's romances are entertaining, for they are full of exciting adventures.
It is nearly half past five, and we cannot reach town before dark.

A comparison of the three forms given above will show clearly the advantage of the first. It is, at least in the examples given, better than the second form, because it suggests the close relationship between the two statements in a way that the second does not attempt, and better than the third, because briefer and therefore more forcible. Indeed, it may be said that this simple method of indicating relationship between statements is one of the most useful devices of composition. The relationship, as above, is commonly one of cause or of consequence.

Note that if the second clause is preceded by an adverb,

such as *accordingly, besides, then, therefore,* or *thus,* and not by a conjunction, the semicolon is still required.

I had never been in the place before; besides, it was dark as a tomb.

Two exceptions to the semicolon rule are worth noting here. First, when clauses are very short, and are alike in form, a comma is usually permissible:

Man proposes, God disposes.
The gates swung apart, the bridge fell, the portcullis was drawn up.

Second, certain colloquialisms are better punctuated with a comma than a semicolon:

I hardly knew him, he was so changed.
Here today, gone tomorrow.

6. *Do not break sentences in two.*
In other words, do not use periods for commas.

I met them on a Cunard liner several years ago. Coming home from Liverpool to New York.
He was an interesting talker. A man who had traveled all over the world and lived in half a dozen countries.

In both these examples, the first period should be replaced by a comma, and the following word begun with a small letter.
It is permissible to make an emphatic word or expression serve the purpose of a sentence and to punctuate it accordingly:

Again and again he called out. No reply.

The writer must, however, be certain that the emphasis is warranted, lest his clipped sentence seem merely a blunder

7

in syntax or in punctuation. Generally speaking, the place for broken sentences is in dialogue, when a character happens to speak in a clipped or fragmentary way.

Rules 3, 4, 5, and 6 cover the most important principles that govern punctuation. They should be so thoroughly mastered that their application becomes second nature.

7. *A participial phrase at the beginning of a sentence must refer to the grammatical subject.*

Walking slowly down the road, he saw a woman accompanied by two children.

The word *walking* refers to the subject of the sentence, not to the woman. If the writer wishes to make it refer to the woman, he must recast the sentence:

He saw a woman, accompanied by two children, walking slowly down the road.

Participial phrases preceded by a conjunction or by a preposition, nouns in apposition, adjectives, and adjective phrases come under the same rule if they begin the sentence. The examples in the left-hand column, below, are wrong; they should be rewritten as shown in the right-hand column.

On arriving in Chicago, his friends met him at the station.	When he arrived (or, On his arrival) in Chicago, his friends met him at the station.
A soldier of proved valor, they entrusted him with the defense of the city.	A soldier of proved valor, he was entrusted with the defense of the city.
Young and inexperienced, the task seemed easy to me.	Young and inexperienced, I thought the task easy.
Without a friend to counsel him, the temptation proved irresistible.	Without a friend to counsel him, he found the temptation irresistible.

8

Sentences violating Rule 7 are often ludicrous:

Being in a dilapidated condition, I was able to buy the house very cheap.
Wondering irresolutely what to do next, the clock struck twelve.

II

Elementary Principles of Composition

8. Choose a suitable design and hold to it.

A basic structural design underlies every kind of writing. The writer will in part follow this design, in part deviate from it, according to his skill, his needs, and the unexpected events that accompany the act of composition. Writing, to be effective, must follow closely the thoughts of the writer, but not necessarily in the order in which those thoughts occur. This calls for a scheme of procedure. In some cases the best design is no design, as with a love letter, which is simply an outpouring, or with a casual essay, which is a ramble. But in most cases, planning must be a deliberate prelude to writing. The first principle of composition, therefore, is to foresee or determine the shape of what is to come and pursue that shape.

A sonnet is built on a fourteen-line frame, of five-foot lines. Hence, the sonneteer knows exactly where he is headed, although he may not know how to get there. Most forms of composition are less clearly defined, more flexible, but all have skeletons to which the writer will bring the flesh and the blood. The more clearly he perceives the shape, the better his chances of success.

9. *Make the paragraph the unit of composition.*

The paragraph is a convenient unit; it serves all forms of literary work. As long as it holds together, a paragraph may be of any length—a single, short sentence or a passage of great duration.

If the subject on which you are writing is of slight extent, or if you intend to treat it briefly, there may be no need of subdividing it into topics. Thus, a brief description, a brief book review, a brief account of a single incident, a narrative merely outlining an action, the setting forth of a single idea —any one of these is best written in a single paragraph. After the paragraph has been written, examine it to see whether subdivision will improve it.

Ordinarily, however, a subject requires subdivision into topics, each of which should be made the subject of a paragraph. The object of treating each topic in a paragraph by itself is, of course, to aid the reader. The beginning of each paragraph is a sign to him that a new step in the development of the subject has been reached.

As a rule, single sentences should not be written or printed as paragraphs. An exception may be made of sentences of transition, indicating the relation between the parts of an exposition or argument.

In dialogue, each speech, even if only a single word, is usually a paragraph by itself; that is, a new paragraph begins with each change of speaker. The application of this rule, when dialogue and narrative are combined, is best learned from examples in well-printed works of fiction. Sometimes a writer, seeking to create an effect of rapid talk, or for some other reason, will elect not to set off each speech in a separate paragraph and instead will run speeches together. The common practice, however, and the one that serves best in most instances, is to give each speech a paragraph of its own.

As a rule, begin each paragraph either with a sentence that suggests the topic or with a sentence that helps the transition. If a paragraph forms part of a larger composition, its relation to what precedes, or its function as a part of the whole, may need to be expressed. This can sometimes be done by a mere word or phrase (*again; therefore; for the same reason*) in the first sentence. Sometimes, however, it is expedient to get into the topic slowly, by way of a sentence or two of introduction or transition.

In narration and description, the paragraph sometimes begins with a concise, comprehensive statement serving to hold together the details that follow.

> The breeze served us admirably.
> The campaign opened with a series of reverses.
> The next ten or twelve pages were filled with a curious set of entries.

But this device, or any device, if too often used, would become a mannerism. More commonly the opening sentence simply indicates by its subject the direction the paragraph is to take.

> At length I thought I might return towards the stockade.
> He picked up the heavy lamp from the table and began to explore.
> Another flight of steps, and they emerged on the roof.

In animated narrative, the paragraphs are likely to be short and without any semblance of a topic sentence, the writer rushing headlong, event following event in rapid succession. The break between such paragraphs merely serves the purpose of a rhetorical pause, throwing into prominence some detail of the action.

In general, remember that paragraphing calls for a good eye, as well as a logical mind. Enormous blocks of print look formidable to a reader. He has a certain reluctance to tackle them; he can lose his way in them. Therefore, breaking long paragraphs in two, even if it is not necessary to do so for sense, meaning, or logical development, is often a visual help. But remember, too, that too many short paragraphs in quick succession can be distracting. Paragraph breaks used only for show read like the writing of commerce or of display advertising. Moderation and a sense of order should be the main considerations in paragraphing.

10. Use the active voice.

The active voice is usually more direct and vigorous than the passive:

I shall always remember my first visit to Boston.

This is much better than

My first visit to Boston will always be remembered by me.

The latter sentence is less direct, less bold, and less concise. If the writer tries to make it more concise by omitting "by me."

My first visit to Boston will always be remembered,

it becomes indefinite: is it the writer, or some person undisclosed, or the world at large, that will always remember this visit?

This rule does not, of course, mean that the writer should entirely discard the passive voice, which is frequently convenient and sometimes necessary.

The dramatists of the Restoration are little esteemed today.
Modern readers have little esteem for the dramatists of the Restoration.

The first would be the preferred form in a paragraph on the dramatists of the Restoration; the second, in a paragraph on the tastes of modern readers. The need of making a particular word the subject of the sentence will often, as in these examples, determine which voice is to be used.

The habitual use of the active voice, however, makes for forcible writing. This is true not only in narrative principally concerned with action, but with writing of any kind. Many a tame sentence of description or exposition can be made lively and emphatic by substituting a transitive in the active voice for some such perfunctory expression as *there is*, or *could be heard*.

There were a great number of dead leaves lying on the ground.	Dead leaves covered the ground.
At dawn the crowing of a rooster could be heard.	The cock's crow came with dawn.
The reason he left college was that his health became impaired.	Failing health compelled him to leave college.
It was not long before he was very sorry that he had said what he had.	He soon repented his words.

Note, in the examples above, that when a sentence is made stronger, it usually becomes shorter. Thus, brevity is a by-product of vigor.

11. Put statements in positive form.

Make definite assertions. Avoid tame, colorless, hesitating, noncommittal language. Use the word *not* as a means of denial or in antithesis, never as a means of evasion.

He was not very often on time.	He usually came late.
He did not think that studying Latin was much use.	He thought the study of Latin useless.
The Taming of the Shrew is rather weak in spots. Shakespeare does not portray Katharine as a very admirable character, nor does Bianca remain long in memory as an important character in Shakespeare's works.	The women in *The Taming of the Shrew* are unattractive. Katharine is disagreeable, Bianca insignificant.

The last example, before correction, is indefinite as well as negative. The corrected version, consequently, is simply a guess at the writer's intention.

All three examples show the weakness inherent in the word *not*. Consciously or unconsciously, the reader is dissatisfied with being told only what is not; he wishes to be told what is. Hence, as a rule, it is better to express even a negative in positive form.

not honest	dishonest
not important	trifling
did not remember	forgot
did not pay any attention to	ignored
did not have much confidence in	distrusted

The antithesis of negative and positive is strong:

Not charity, but simple justice.
Not that I loved Caesar less, but that I loved Rome more.

Negative words other than *not* are usually strong.

Her loveliness I never knew/Until she smiled on me.

12. Use definite, specific, concrete language.

Prefer the specific to the general, the definite to the vague, the concrete to the abstract.

A period of unfavorable weather set in.	It rained every day for a week.
He showed satisfaction as he took possession of his well-earned reward.	He grinned as he pocketed the coin.

If those who have studied the art of writing are in accord on any one point, it is on this: the surest way to arouse and hold the attention of the reader is by being specific, definite, and concrete. The greatest writers—Homer, Dante, Shakespeare—are effective largely because they deal in particulars and report the details that matter. Their words call up pictures.

Willa Cather, to cite a modern author, demonstrates in her introduction to *My Ántonia* how prose is made vivid by the use of words that evoke images and sensations:

Last summer, in a season of intense heat, Jim Burden and I happened to be crossing Iowa on the same train. He and I are old friends, we grew up together in the same Nebraska town, and we had a great deal to say to each other. While the train flashed through never-ending miles of ripe wheat, by country towns and bright-flowered pastures and oak groves wilting in the sun, we sat in the observation car, where the woodwork was hot to the touch and red dust lay deep over everything. The dust and heat, the burning wind, reminded us of many things. We were talking about what it is like to spend one's childhood in little towns like these, buried in wheat and corn, under stimulating extremes of climate: burning summers when the world lies green and billowy beneath a brilliant sky, when one is fairly stifled in vegetation, in the colour and smell of strong weeds and heavy harvests; blustery winters with little snow, when the whole country is stripped bare and grey as sheet-iron. We agreed that no one who had not grown up in a little prairie town could know anything about it. It was a kind of freemasonry, we said.[1]

If the experiences of Jim Hawkins and of David Balfour, of Kim, of Nostromo, have seemed for the moment real to countless readers, if in reading Carlyle we have almost the sense of being present at the taking of the Bastille, it is because the details used are definite, the terms concrete. It is not that every detail is given—that would be impossible, as well as to no purpose—but that all the significant details are given, and with such accuracy and vigor that the reader, in imagination, can project himself into the scene.

[1] *My Antonia* by Willa Cather, copyright 1918 by Houghton Mifflin Company. Reprinted by permission of the publisher.

In exposition and in argument, the writer must likewise never lose his hold upon the concrete, and even when he is dealing with general principles, he must give particular instances of their application.

In his *Philosophy of Style*, Herbert Spencer gives two sentences to illustrate how the vague and general can be turned into the vivid and particular:

In proportion as the manners, customs, and amusements of a nation are cruel and barbarous, the regulations of their penal code will be severe.

In proportion as men delight in battles, bull-fights, and combats of gladiators, will they punish by hanging, burning and the rack.

To show what happens when strong writing is deprived of its vigor, George Orwell once took a passage from the Bible and drained it of its blood. On the left, below, is Orwell's translation; on the right, the verse from Ecclesiastes.

Objective consideration of contemporary phenomena compels the conclusion that success or failure in competitive activities exhibits no tendency to be commensurate with innate capacity, but that a considerable element of the unpredictable must inevitably be taken into account.

I returned, and saw under the sun, that the race is not to the swift, nor the battle to the strong, neither yet bread to the wise, nor yet riches to men of understanding, nor yet favor to men of skill; but time and chance happeneth to them all.

13. *Omit needless words.*

Vigorous writing is concise. A sentence should contain no unnecessary words, a paragraph no unnecessary sentences, for the same reason that a drawing should have no unnecessary lines and a machine no unnecessary parts. This requires not that the writer make all his sentences short, or that he avoid all detail and treat his subjects only in outline, but that every word tell.

Many expressions in common use violate this principle:

the question as to whether	whether (the question whether)
there is no doubt but that	no doubt (doubtless)
used for fuel purposes	used for fuel
he is a man who	he
in a hasty manner	hastily
this is a subject that	this subject
His story is a strange one.	His story is strange.

An expression that is especially debilitating is *the fact that*. It should be revised out of every sentence in which it occurs.

owing to the fact that	since (because)
in spite of the fact that	though (although)
call your attention to the fact that	remind you (notify you)
I was unaware of the fact that	I was unaware that (did not know)
the fact that he had not succeeded	his failure
the fact that I had arrived	my arrival

See also under the words *case, character, nature* in Chapter IV.

Who is, which was, and the like are often superfluous.

His brother, who is a member of the same firm	His brother, a member of the same firm
Trafalgar, which was Nelson's last battle	Trafalgar, Nelson's last battle

As positive statement is more concise than negative, and the active voice more concise than the passive, many of the examples given under Rules 10 and 11 illustrate this rule as well.

A common way to fall into wordiness is to present a single

complex idea, step by step, in a series of sentences that might to advantage be combined into one.

Macbeth was very ambitious. This led him to wish to become king of Scotland. The witches told him that this wish of his would come true. The king of Scotland at this time was Duncan. Encouraged by his wife, Macbeth murdered Duncan. He was thus enabled to succeed Duncan as king. (51 words.)

Encouraged by his wife, Macbeth achieved his ambition and realized the prediction of the witches by murdering Duncan and becoming king of Scotland in his place. (26 words.)

14. Avoid a succession of loose sentences.

This rule refers especially to loose sentences of a particular type: those consisting of two co-ordinate clauses, the second introduced by a conjunction or relative. Although single sentences of this type may be unobjectionable (see under Rule 4), a series soon becomes monotonous and tedious.

An unskillful writer will sometimes construct a whole paragraph of sentences of this kind, using as connectives *and, but,* and less frequently, *who, which, when, where,* and *while,* these last in nonrestrictive senses (see under Rule 3).

The third concert of the subscription series was given last evening, and a large audience was in attendance. Mr. Edward Appleton was the soloist, and the Boston Symphony Orchestra furnished the instrumental music. The former showed himself to be an artist of the first rank, while the latter proved itself fully deserving of its high reputation. The interest aroused by the series has been very gratifying to the Committee, and it is planned to give a similar series annually hereafter. The fourth concert will be given on Tuesday, May 10, when an equally attractive program will be presented.

Apart from its triteness and emptiness, the paragraph above is bad because of the structure of its sentences, with their mechanical symmetry and sing-song. Contrast with them these sentences from the chapter "What I Believe" in E. M. Forster's *Two Cheers for Democracy:*

I believe in aristocracy, though—if that is the right word, and if a democrat may use it. Not an aristocracy of power, based upon rank and influence, but an aristocracy of the sensitive, the considerate and the plucky. Its members are to be found in all nations and classes, and all through the ages, and there is a secret understanding between them when they meet. They represent the true human tradition, the one permanent victory of our queer race over cruelty and chaos. Thousands of them perish in obscurity, a few are great names. They are sensitive for others as well as for themselves, they are considerate without being fussy, their pluck is not swankiness but the power to endure, and they can take a joke.[2]

If the writer finds that he has written a series of loose sentences, he should recast enough of them to remove the monotony, replacing them by simple sentences, by sentences of two clauses joined by a semicolon, by periodic sentences of two clauses, by sentences (loose or periodic) of three clauses—whichever best represent the real relations of the thought.

15. *Express co-ordinate ideas in similar form.*

This principle, that of parallel construction, requires that expressions similar in content and function be outwardly similar. The likeness of form enables the reader to recognize more readily the likeness of content and function. The Beatitudes and the petitions of the Lord's Prayer are familiar instances of the virtue of parallel construction.

Blessed are the poor in spirit: for theirs is the kingdom of heaven.

[2] From *Two Cheers for Democracy,* coyright, 1951, by E. M. Forster. Published by Harcourt, Brace and Company, Inc.

Blessed are they that mourn: for they shall be comforted.

Blessed are the meek: for they shall inherit the earth.

Blessed are they which do hunger and thirst after righteousness: for they shall be filled.

Our Father, which art in heaven, Hallowed be thy name. Thy kingdom come. Thy will be done in earth, as it is in heaven. Give us this day our daily bread. And forgive us our debts, as we forgive our debtors. And lead us not into temptation, but deliver us from evil: For thine is the kingdom, and the power, and the glory, for ever.

The unskillful writer often violates this principle, from a mistaken belief that he should constantly vary the form of his expressions. It is true that in repeating a statement in order to emphasize it he may have need to vary its form. But apart from this, he should follow the principle of parallel construction.

| Formerly, science was taught by the textbook method, while now the laboratory method is employed. | Formerly, science was taught by the textbook method; now it is taught by the laboratory method. |

The left-hand version gives the impression that the writer is undecided or timid; he seems unable or afraid to choose one form of expression and hold to it. The right-hand version shows that the writer has at least made his choice and abided by it.

By this principle, an article or a preposition applying to all the members of a series must either be used only before the first term or else be repeated before each term.

| The French, the Italians, Spanish, and Portuguese | The French, the Italians, the Spanish, and the Portuguese |
| In spring, summer, or in winter | In spring, summer, or winter (In spring, in summer, or in winter) |

Correlative expressions (*both, and; not, but; not only, but also; either, or; first, second, third;* and the like) should be followed by the same grammatical construction. Many violations of this rule can be corrected by rearranging the sentence.

It was both a long ceremony and very tedious.	The ceremony was both long and tedious.
A time not for words but action.	A time not for words but for action.
Either you must grant his request or incur his ill will.	You must either grant his request or incur his ill will.
My objections are, first, the injustice of the measure; second, that it is unconstitutional.	My objections are, first, that the measure is unjust; second, that it is unconstitutional.

It may be asked, what if a writer needs to express a rather large number of similar ideas, say twenty? Must he write twenty consecutive sentences of the same pattern? On closer examination he will probably find that the difficulty is imaginary, that his twenty ideas can be classified in groups, and that he need apply the principle only within each group. Otherwise he had best avoid the difficulty by putting his statements in the form of a table.

16. Keep related words together.

The position of the words in a sentence is the principal means of showing their relationship. Confusion and ambi-guity result when words are badly placed. The writer must, therefore, so far as possible, bring together the words, and groups of words, that are related in thought, and keep apart those that are not so related.

He noticed a large stain in the rug that was right in the center.	He noticed a large stain right in the center of the rug.

In the left-hand version, the reader has no way of knowing whether the stain was in the center of the rug or the rug was in the center of the room.

The subject of a sentence and the principal verb should not, as a rule, be separated by a phrase or clause that can be transferred to the beginning.

Wordsworth, in the fifth book of *The Excursion,* gives a minute description of this church.	In the fifth book of *The Excursion,* Wordsworth gives a minute description of this church.
A dog, if you fail to discipline him, becomes a household pest.	Unless disciplined, a dog becomes a household pest.

The objection is that the interposed phrase or clause needlessly interrupts the flow of the main clause. This objection, however, does not usually hold when the flow is interrupted only by a relative clause or by an expression in apposition. Nor does it hold in periodic sentences in which the interruption is a deliberate device for creating suspense (see examples under Rule 18).

The relative pronoun should come, as a rule, immediately after its antecedent.

There was a stir in the audience that suggested disapproval.	A stir that suggested disapproval swept the audience.
He wrote three articles about his adventures in Spain, which were published in *Harper's Magazine.*	He published three articles in *Harper's Magazine* about his adventures in Spain.
This is a portrait of Benjamin Harrison, grandson of William Henry Harrison, who became President in 1889.	This is a portrait of Benjamin Harrison, grandson of William Henry Harrison. He became President in 1889.

If the antecedent consists of a group of words, the relative comes at the end of the group, unless this would cause ambiguity.

The Superintendent of the Chicago Division, who

No ambiguity results from the above. But,

A proposal to amend the Sherman Act, which has been variously judged

leaves the reader wondering whether it is the proposal or the Act that has been variously judged. The relative clause must be moved forward, to read: "A proposal, which has been variously judged, to amend the Sherman Act. . ." Similarly,

The grandson of William Henry Harrison, who	William Henry Harrison's grandson, Benjamin Harrison, who

A noun in apposition may come between antecedent and relative, because in such a combination no real ambiguity can arise.

The Duke of York, his brother, who was regarded with hostility by the Whigs

Modifiers should come, if possible, next to the word they modify. If several expressions modify the same word, they should be so arranged that no wrong relation is suggested.

All the members were not present.	Not all the members were present.
He only found two mistakes.	He found only two mistakes.

24

The chairman said he hoped all members would give generously to the Fund at a meeting of the committee yesterday.	At a meeting of the committee yesterday, the chairman said he hoped all members would give generously to the Fund.
Major R. E. Joyce will give a lecture on Tuesday evening in Bailey Hall, to which the public is invited on "My Experiences in Mesopotamia" at eight P.M.	On Tuesday evening at eight P.M., Major R. E. Joyce will give a lecture in Bailey Hall on "My Experiences in Mesopotamia." The public is invited.

Note, in the last example, how swiftly meaning departs when words are wrongly juxtaposed.

17. In summaries, keep to one tense.

In summarizing the action of a drama, the writer should use the present tense. In summarizing a poem, story, or novel, he should use the present, though he may use the past if it seems more natural to do so. If the summary is in the present tense, antecedent action should be expressed by the perfect; if in the past, by the past perfect.

Chance prevents Friar John from delivering Friar Lawrence's letter to Romeo. Meanwhile, owing to her father's arbitrary change of the day set for her wedding, Juliet has been compelled to drink the potion on Tuesday night, with the result that Balthasar informs Romeo of her supposed death before Friar Lawrence learns of the nondelivery of the letter.

But whichever tense is used in the summary, a past tense in indirect discourse or in indirect question remains unchanged.

The Friar confesses that it was he who married them.

Apart from the exceptions noted, whichever tense the writer chooses he should use throughout. Shifting from one tense to the other gives the appearance of uncertainty and irresolution.

In presenting the statements or the thought of some one else, as in summarizing an essay or reporting a speech, the writer should not overwork such expressions as "he said," "he stated," "the speaker added," "the speaker then went on to say," "the author also thinks," or the like. He should indicate clearly at the outset, once for all, that what follows is summary, and then waste no words in repeating the notification.

In notebooks, in newspapers, in handbooks of literature, summaries of one kind or another may be indispensable, and for children in primary schools it is a useful exercise to retell a story in their own words. But in the criticism or interpretation of literature the writer should be careful to avoid dropping into summary. He may find it necessary to devote one or two sentences to indicating the subject, or the opening situation, of the work he is discussing; he may cite numerous details to illustrate its qualities. But he should aim to write an orderly discussion supported by evidence, not a summary with occasional comment. Similarly, if the scope of his discussion includes a number of works, he will as a rule do better not to take them up singly in chronological order, but to aim from the beginning at establishing general conclusions.

18. Place the emphatic words of a sentence at the end.

The proper place in the sentence for the word or group of words that the writer desires to make most prominent is usually the end.

Humanity has hardly advanced in fortitude since that time, though it has advanced in many other ways.	Humanity, since that time, has advanced in many other ways, but it has hardly advanced in fortitude.
This steel is principally used for making razors, because of its hardness.	Because of its hardness, this steel is principally used in making razors.

26

The word or group of words entitled to this position of prominence is usually the logical predicate, that is, the *new* element in the sentence, as it is in the second example.

The effectiveness of the periodic sentence arises from the prominence it gives to the main statement.

Four centuries ago, Christopher Columbus, one of the Italian mariners whom the decline of their own republics had put at the service of the world and of adventure, seeking for Spain a westward passage to the Indies as a set-off against the achievements of Portuguese discoverers, lighted on America.

With these hopes and in this belief I would urge you, laying aside all hindrance, thrusting away all private aims, to devote yourself unswervingly and unflinchingly to the vigorous and successful prosecution of this war.

The other prominent position in the sentence is the beginning. Any element in the sentence, other than the subject, becomes emphatic when placed first.

Deceit or treachery he could never forgive.
So vast and rude, fretted by the action of nearly three thousand years, the fragments of this architecture may often seem, at first sight, like works of nature.
Home is the sailor.

A subject coming first in its sentence may be emphatic, but hardly by its position alone. In the sentence,

Great kings worshiped at his shrine,

the emphasis upon *kings* arises largely from its meaning and from the context. To receive special emphasis, the subject of a sentence must take the position of the predicate.

Through the middle of the valley flowed a winding stream.

The principle that the proper place for what is to be made most prominent is the end applies equally to the words of a sentence, to the sentences of a paragraph, and to the paragraphs of a composition.

III

A Few Matters of Form

Colloquialisms. If you use a colloquialism, or a slang word or phrase, simply use it; do not draw attention to it by enclosing it in quotation marks. To do so is to put on airs, as though you were inviting the reader to join you in a select society of those who know better.

Exclamations. Do not attempt to emphasize simple statements by using a mark of exclamation.

It was a wonderful show!   It was a wonderful show.

The exclamation mark is to be reserved for use after true exclamations or commands.

What a wonderful show!
Halt!

Headings. It is usually best to leave plenty of space at the top of Page 1 of a manuscript. Place the heading, or title, at least a fourth of the way down the page. Leave a blank line, or its equivalent in space, after the heading. On succeeding pages, begin near the top, but not so near as to give a crowded appearance. Omit the period after a title or heading. A question mark or an exclamation point may be used if the heading calls for it.

Margins. Keep right-hand and left-hand margins roughly the same width. Exception: If a great deal of annotating or editing is anticipated, the left-hand margin should be roomy enough to accommodate this work.

Numerals. Do not spell out dates or other serial numbers. Write them in figures or in Roman notation, as may be appropriate.

August 9, 1918   Chapter XII
Rule 3   352d Infantry

Exception: Spell out dates and numbers when they occur in speech.

"I arrived home on August ninth."

Parentheses. A sentence containing an expression in parentheses is punctuated, outside of the marks of parenthesis, exactly as if the parenthetical expression were absent. The expression within the marks is punctuated as if it stood by itself, except that the final stop is omitted unless it is a question mark or an exclamation point.

I went to his house yesterday (my third attempt to see him), but he had left town.
He declares (and why should we doubt his good faith?) that he is now certain of success.

(When a wholly detached expression or sentence is parenthesized, the final stop comes before the last mark of parenthesis.)

Quotations. Formal quotations, cited as documentary evidence, are introduced by a colon and enclosed in quotation marks.

The United States Coast Pilot has this to say of the place: "Bracy Cove, 0.5 mile eastward of Bear Island, is exposed to southeast winds, has a rocky and uneven bottom, and is unfit for anchorage."

A quotation grammatically in apposition or the direct object of a verb is preceded by a comma and enclosed in quotation marks.

I am reminded of the advice of my neighbor, "Never worry about your heart till it stops beating."
Mark Twain says, "A classic is something that everybody wants to have read and nobody wants to read."

When a quotation is followed by an attributive phrase, the comma is enclosed within the quotation marks.

"I can't attend," she said.

Typographical usage dictates that the comma be inside the marks, though logically it often seems not to belong there.

"The Clerks," "Luke Havergal," and "Richard Cory" are in Robinson's *Children of the Night*.

When quotations of an entire line, or more, of either verse or prose, are begun on a fresh line and indented, they need not be enclosed in quotation marks.

Wordsworth's enthusiasm for the Revolution was at first unbounded:

> Bliss was it in that dawn to be alive,
> But to be young was very heaven!

Quotations introduced by *that* are regarded as in indirect discourse and not enclosed in quotation marks.

Keats declares that beauty is truth, truth beauty.

Proverbial expressions and familiar phrases of literary origin require no quotation marks.

> These are the times that try men's souls.
> He lives far from the madding crowd.

References. In scholarly work requiring exact references, abbreviate titles that occur frequently, giving the full forms in an alphabetical list at the end. As a general practice, give the references in parentheses or in footnotes, not in the body of the sentence. Omit the words *act, scene, line, book, volume, page,* except when referring by only one of them. Punctuate as indicated below.

In the second scene of the third act.	In III.ii (still better, simply insert III.ii in parentheses at the proper place in the sentence)

After the killing of Polonius, Hamlet is placed under guard (IV.ii. 14).

2 Samuel i: 17–27

Othello II.iii. 264–267, III.iii. 155–161.

Syllabication. If there is room at the end of a line for one or more syllables of a word, but not for the whole word, divide the word, unless this involves cutting off only a single letter, or cutting off only two letters of a long word. No hard and fast rule for all words can be laid down. The principles most frequently applicable are:

(a) Divide the word according to its formation:

know-ledge (not knowl-edge); Shake-speare (not Shakes-peare); de-scribe (not des-cribe);

(b) Divide on the vowel:

edi-ble (not ed-ible); propo-sition; ordi-nary; espe-cial; religious; oppo-nents; regu-lar; classi-fi-ca-tion (three divisions allowable); deco-rative; presi-dent;

(c) Divide between double letters, unless they come at the end of the simple form of the word:

Apen-nines; Cincin-nati; refer-ring; but tell-ing

(d) Do not divide before final *-ed* if the *e* is silent:

treat-ed (but not roam-ed or nam-ed)

The treatment of consonants in combination is best shown from examples:

atmos-phere; for-tune; pic-ture; sin-gle; presump-tuous; illus-tration; sub-stan-tial (either division); indus-try; instruc-tion; sug-ges-tion; incen-diary.

The student will do well to examine the syllable-division in a number of pages of any carefully printed book. When in doubt, consult a dictionary.

Titles. For the titles of literary works, scholarly usage prefers italics with capitalized initials. The usage of editors and publishers varies, some using italics with capitalized initials, others using Roman with capitalized initials and with or without quotation marks. Use italics (indicated in manuscript by underscoring) except in writing for a periodical that follows a different practice. Omit initial *A* or *The* from titles when you place the possessive before them.

A Tale of Two Cities; Dickens's Tale of Two Cities.

IV

Words and Expressions
Commonly Misused

MANY OF THE words and expressions here listed are not so much bad English as bad style, the commonplaces of careless writing. As illustrated under *Feature*, the proper correction is likely to be not the replacement of one word or set of words by another, but the replacement of vague generality by definite statement.

The shape of our language is not rigid; in questions of usage we have no lawgiver whose word is final. Students whose curiosity is aroused by the interpretations that follow, or whose doubts are raised, will wish to pursue their investigations further. Books useful in such pursuits are: *The American College Dictionary, Webster's New Collegiate Dictionary, Webster's New World Dictionary of the American Language,* Margaret Nicholson's *Dictionary of American-English Usage.*

Aforesaid. Useful in legal phrasing, damaging in standard prose. Write *named above,* or *mentioned earlier.*

All right. Idiomatic in familiar speech as a detached phrase in the sense, "Agreed," or "Go ahead," or "O.K."

33

Always written as two words; there is no such word as *alright*.

Allude. Do not confuse with *elude*. You *allude* to a book; you *elude* a pursuer. Note, too, that *allude* is not synonymous with *refer*. An allusion is an indirect mention, a reference is a specific one.

Allusion. Easily confused with *illusion*. The first means "an indirect reference"; the second means "an unreal image" or "a false impression."

And/or. A device borrowed from legal writing. It destroys the flow and goodness of a sentence. Useful only to those who need to write diagrammatically or enjoy writing in riddles.

Anybody. In the sense of *any person* not to be written as two words. "Any body" means *any corpse*, or *any human form*, or *any group*. The rule holds equally for *everybody, nobody,* and *somebody*.

Anyone. In the sense of *anybody* best written as one word. "Any one" might mean *any single person* or *any single thing*.

As good or better than. Expressions of this type should be corrected by rearranging the sentences.

My opinion is as good or better than his.	My opinion is as good as his, or better (if not better).

As to whether. *Whether* is sufficient.
At. Not to follow *where*.

Where is your luggage at?	Where is your luggage?

But. Unnecessary after *doubt* and *help*.

I have no doubt but that	I have no doubt that
He could not help but see that	He could not help seeing that

34

The too frequent use of *but* as a conjunction leads to the fault discussed under Rule 14. A loose sentence formed with *but* can always be converted into a periodic sentence formed with *although*, as illustrated under Rule 4.

Particularly awkward is one *but* closely following another, thus making a contrast to a contrast, or a reservation to a reservation. This is easily corrected by rearrangement.

| America had vast resources, but she seemed almost wholly unprepared for war. But within a year she had created an army of four million men. | America seemed almost wholly unprepared for war, but she had vast resources. Within a year she had created an army of four million men. |

Can. Means *am (is, are) able.* Not to be used as a substitute for *may.*

Can't hardly. An unintentional double negative. The correct phrase is *can hardly,* or *can scarcely.*

Case. Often unnecessary.

| In many cases, the rooms were poorly ventilated. | Many of the rooms were poorly ventilated. |
| It has rarely been the case that any mistake has been made. | Few mistakes have been made. |

Certainly. Used indiscriminately by some writers, much as others use *very,* in an attempt to intensify any and every statement. A mannerism of this kind, bad in speech, is even worse in writing.

Character. Often simply redundant, used from a mere habit of wordiness.

| Acts of a hostile character. | Hostile acts. |

Claim, vb. With object-noun, means *lay claim to.* May be used with a dependent clause if this sense is clearly involved: "He claimed that he was the sole surviving heir." (But even here, "claimed to be" would be better.) Not to be used as a substitute for *declare, maintain,* or *charge.*

He claimed he knew how.   He declared he knew how.

Clever. This word has been greatly overworked; it is best restricted to ingenuity displayed in small matters. Note also that the word means one thing when applied to men, another when applied to horses. A clever horse is a good-natured one, not an ingenious one.

Compare. To *compare to* is to point out or imply resemblances, between objects regarded as essentially of different order; to *compare with* is mainly to point out differences, between objects regarded as essentially of the same order. Thus, life has been compared to a pilgrimage, to a drama, to a battle; Congress may be compared with the British Parliament. Paris has been compared to ancient Athens; it may be compared with modern London.

Comprise. Literally, *embrace.* A zoo *comprises* mammals, reptiles, and birds (because it embraces, or includes, them). But animals do not comprise (embrace) a zoo—they *constitute* a zoo.

Consider. Not followed by *as* when it means "believe to be." "I consider him thoroughly competent." Compare, "The lecturer considered Cromwell first as soldier and second as administrator." Here, "considered" means "examined" or "discussed."

Contact. As a transitive verb, the word is vague and self-important. Do not *contact* anybody; get in touch with him, or look him up, or phone him, or find him, or meet him.

Data. A plural, like *phenomena* and *strata.*

Different than. Here logic supports established usage: one thing differs *from* another, hence, *different from.* Or, *other than, unlike.*

Disinterested. Avoid in the sense of *uninterested.* Today chiefly used to mean *impartial.*

Divided into. Not to be misused for *composed of*. The line is sometimes difficult to draw; doubtless plays are divided into acts, but poems are composed of stanzas. An apple, halved, is divided into sections; but an apple is composed of seeds, flesh, and skin.

Don't. Contraction of *do not*. The contraction of *does not* is *doesn't*.

Due to. Loosely used for *through, because of,* or *owing to,* in adverbial phrases.

He lost the first game due to carelessness.	He lost the first game because of carelessness.

In correct use related as predicate or as modifier to a particular noun: "This invention is due to Edison"; "losses due to preventable fires."

Effect. As noun, means *result*; as verb, means to *bring about, accomplish* (not to be confused with *affect,* which means "to influence").

As noun, often loosely used in perfunctory writing about fashions, music, painting, and other arts: "an Oriental effect"; "effects in pale green"; "very delicate effects"; "subtle effects"; "a charming effect was produced by." The writer who has a definite meaning to express will not take refuge in such vagueness.

Enormity. Use only in the sense *monstrous wickedness*. Misleading, if not wrong, when used to express bigness.

Enthuse. A colloquial verb, unacceptable in formal writing.

She was enthused about her new car.	She was enthusiastic about her new car.
She enthused about her new car.	She talked enthusiastically (or expressed enthusiasm) about her new car.

Etc. Literally, *and other things*; sometimes loosely used to mean *and other persons*. The phrase is equivalent to *and* *the rest, and so forth,* and hence is not to be used if one of these would be insufficient, that is, if the reader would be left in doubt as to any important particulars. Least open to objection when it represents the last terms of a list already given almost in full, or immaterial words at the end of a quotation.

At the end of a list introduced by *such as, for example,* or any similar expression, *etc.* is incorrect.

Fact. Use this word only of matters of a kind capable of direct verification, not of matters of judgment. That a particular event happened on a given date, that lead melts at a certain temperature, are facts. But such conclusions as that Napoleon was the greatest of modern generals, or that the climate of California is delightful, however incontestable they may be, are not properly called facts.

Factor. A hackneyed word; the expressions of which it forms part can usually be replaced by something more direct and idiomatic.

His superior training was the great factor in his winning the match.	He won the match by being better trained.
Air power is becoming an increasingly important factor in deciding battles.	Air power is playing a larger and larger part in deciding battles.

Farther, further. The two words are commonly interchanged, but there is a distinction worth observing: *farther* serves best as a distance word, *further* as a time or quantity word. You chase a ball *farther* than the other fellow; you pursue a subject *further*.

Feature. Another hackneyed word; like *factor* it usually adds nothing to the sentence in which it occurs.

A feature of the entertainment especially worthy of mention was the singing of Miss A.	(Better use the same number of words to tell what Miss A. sang and how she sang it.)

As a verb, in the sense of *offer as a special attraction*, to be avoided.

Fix. Colloquial in America for *arrange, prepare, mend.* The usage is well established. But bear in mind that this verb is from *figere: to make firm, to place definitely.* These are the preferred meanings of the word.

Folk. A collective noun, equivalent to *people.* Use the singular form only. *Folks,* in the sense of *parents, family, those present,* is colloquial and too folksy for ordinary usage.

Her folks arrived by the afternoon train.	Her father and mother arrived by the afternoon train.

Get. The colloquial *have got* for *have* should not be used in writing. The preferable form of the participle is *got,* not *gotten.*

He has not got any sense.	He has no sense.
They returned without having gotten any.	They returned without having got any.

He is a man who. A common type of redundant expression; see Rule 13.

He is a man who is very ambitious.	He is very ambitious.
Vermont is a state that attracts visitors because of its winter sports.	Vermont attracts visitors because of its winter sports.

However. Avoid starting a sentence with *however* when the meaning is *nevertheless.* The word usually serves better when not in first position.

The roads were almost impassable. However, we at last succeeded in reaching camp.	The roads were almost impassable. At last, however, we succeeded in reaching camp.

When *however* comes first, it means *in whatever way* or *to whatever extent.*

However you advise him, he will probably do as he thinks best.
However discouraging the prospect, he never lost heart.

Illusion. See *allusion.*
Imply. Infer. Not interchangeable.

Farming implies early rising.
Since he was a farmer, we inferred that he got up early.

Inside of, inside. The *of* following *inside* is correct in the adverbial meaning *in less than.* In other meanings *of* is un-necessary.

Inside of five minutes I'll be inside the bank.

Interesting. An unconvincing word; avoid it as a means of introduction. Instead of announcing that what you are about to tell is interesting, make it so.

An interesting story is told of	(Tell the story without preamble.)
In connection with the forthcoming visit of Mr. B. to America, it is interesting to recall that he	Mr. B., who will soon visit America

Also to be avoided in introduction is the word *funny.* Nothing becomes funny by being labelled so.
In the last analysis. A bankrupt expression.
Irregardless. Should be *regardless.* The error results from failure to see the negative in *-less,* and from a desire to get it in as a prefix, suggested by such words as *irregular, irresponsible,* and, perhaps especially, *irrespective.*

Kind of. Except in familiar style not to be used as a substitute for *rather* or *something like*. Restrict it to its literal sense: "Amber is a kind of fossil resin"; "I dislike that kind of notoriety." The same holds true of *sort of*.

Lay. Except in slang ("Let it lay"), do not misuse for *lie*. The hen, or the play, *lays* an egg; the llama *lies* down. The playwright went home and *lay* down.

> Lie ; lay; lain; lying
> Lay; laid; laid; laying

Leave. Not to be misused for *let*.

Leave it stand the way it is.	Let it stand the way it is.
Leave go of that rope!	Let go of that rope!

Less. Should not be misused for *fewer*.

He had less men than in the previous campaign.	He had fewer men than in the previous campaign.

Less refers to quantity, *fewer* to number. "His troubles are less than mine" means "His troubles are not so great as mine." "His troubles are fewer than mine" means "His troubles are not so numerous as mine."

Like. Not to be used for *as*. *Like* governs nouns and pronouns; before phrases and clauses the equivalent word is *as*.

We spent the evening like in the old days.	We spent the evening as in the old days.
Chloë smells good, like a pretty girl should.	Chloë smells good, as a pretty girl should.

The use of *like* for *as* has its defenders; they argue that any usage that achieves currency becomes valid automatically. This, they say, is the way the language is formed. It is and it isn't. An expression sometimes merely enjoys a vogue, much as an article of apparel does. *Like* has always been widely misused by the illiterate; lately it has been taken up by the knowing and the well-informed, who find it catchy, or liberating, and who use it as though they were slumming. If every word or device that achieved currency were immediately authenticated, simply on the grounds of popularity, the language would be as chaotic as a ball game with no foul lines. For the student, perhaps the most useful thing to know about *like* is that most carefully edited publications regard its use before phrases and clauses as simple error.

Line, along these lines. *Line* in the sense of *course of procedure, conduct, thought,* is allowable, but has been so much overworked, particularly in the phrase *along these lines,* that a writer who aims at freshness or originality had better discard it entirely.

Mr. B. also spoke along the same lines.	Mr. B. also spoke, to the same effect.
He is studying along the line of French literature.	He is studying French literature.

Literal, literally. Often incorrectly used in support of exaggeration or violent metaphor.

A literal flood of abuse	A flood of abuse
Literally dead with fatigue	Almost dead with fatigue (dead tired)

Loan. As a verb, prefer *lend*.

Lend me your ears.
The loan of your ears

Me. Use it confidently. Never substitute *I* as object of a verb or preposition in the hope of achieving elegance.

Between you and I	Between you and me
They came to meet my wife and I.	They came to meet my wife and me.

Most. Not to be used for *almost.*

Most everybody	Almost everybody
Most all the time	Almost all the time

Nature. Often simply redundant, used like *character.*

Acts of a hostile nature	Hostile acts

Often vaguely used in such expressions as "a lover of nature"; "poems about nature." Unless more specific statements follow, the reader cannot tell whether the poems have to do with natural scenery, rural life, the sunset, the untracked wilderness, or the habits of squirrels.

None. Takes the singular verb. The rule applies equally to other distributive expressions: *each, each one, everybody, everyone, many a man, nobody.*

None of us are perfect.	None of us is perfect.
Everybody thinks they have a sense of humor.	Everybody thinks he has a sense of humor.

Oftentimes, ofttimes. Archaic forms, no longer in good use. The modern word is *often.*

One of the most. Avoid this feeble formula. "One of the most interesting developments of modern science is, etc."; "Switzerland is one of the most interesting countries of Europe." There is nothing wrong in this; it is simply threadbare.

A common blunder is to use a singular verb in a relative clause following this or a similar expression, when the relative is the subject.

One of the ablest men that has attacked this problem	One of the ablest men that have attacked this problem

Participle for verbal noun.

Do you mind me asking a question?	Do you mind my asking a question?
There was little prospect of the Senate accepting even this compromise.	There was little prospect of the Senate's accepting even this compromise.

In the left-hand column, *asking* and *accepting* are present participles; in the right-hand column, they are verbal nouns (gerunds). The construction shown in the left-hand column is occasionally found, and has its defenders. Yet it is easy to see that the second sentence has to do not with a prospect of the Senate, but with a prospect of accepting. In this example, at least, the construction is plainly illogical.

Any sentence in which the use of the possessive is awkward or impossible should of course be recast.

In the event of a reconsideration of the whole matter's becoming necessary	If it should become necessary to reconsider the whole matter
There was great dissatisfaction with the decision of the arbitrators being favorable to the company.	There was great dissatisfaction that the arbitrators should have decided in favor of the company.

People. A word with many meanings (Webster gives nine). *The people* is a political term, not to be confused with *the public*. From the people comes political support or opposition; from the public comes artistic appreciation or commercial patronage.

The word *people* is best not used with words of number, in place of *persons*. If of "six people" five went away, how many "people" would be left? Answer: one people.

Personalize. A pretentious word, often carrying bad advice. Do not *personalize* your prose; simply make it good and keep it clean. See Chapter V, Reminder 1.

A highly personalized affair	A highly personal affair
Personalize your stationery	Get up a letterhead

Personally. Often unnecessary.

| Personally, I thought it was a good book. | I thought it a good book. |

Phase. Means a stage of transition or development: "the phases of the moon"; "the last phase." Not to be used for *aspect* or *topic*.

| Another phase of the subject | Another point (another question) |

Possess. Often used because to the writer it sounds more impressive than *have* or *own.* Such use is not incorrect, but is to be guarded against.

| He possessed great courage. | He had great courage (was very brave). |
| He was the fortunate possessor of | He was lucky enough to own |

Prove. The past participle is *proved.*
Refer. See *allude.*
Respective, respectively. These words may usually be omitted with advantage.

| Works of fiction are listed under the names of their respective authors. | Works of fiction are listed under the names of their authors. |
| The mile run and the two-mile run were won by Jones and Cummings respectively. | The mile run was won by Jones; the two-mile run by Cummings. |

Shall, will. In formal writing, the future tense requires *shall* for the first person, *will* for the second and third. The formula to express the speaker's belief regarding his future action or state is *I shall; I will* expresses his determination or his consent. A swimmer in distress cries, "I shall drown; no one will save me!" A suicide puts it the other way, "I will drown; no one shall save me!" In relaxed speech, however, the words *shall* and *will* are seldom used precisely—our ear guides us, or fails to guide us, as the case may be, and we are quite likely to drown when we want to survive, and survive when we want to drown.

Should. See under Would.

So. Avoid, in writing, the use of *so* as an intensifier: "so good"; "so warm"; "so delightful."

Sort of. See under *Kind of.*

Split infinitive. There is precedent from the fourteenth century downward for interposing an adverb between *to* and the infinitive it governs, but the construction is for the most part avoided by the careful writer.

To diligently inquire	To inquire diligently

For another side to the split infinitive, see under Chapter V, Reminder 14.

State. Not to be used as a mere substitute for *say, remark.* Restrict it to the sense of *express fully or clearly,* as, "He refused to state his objections."

Student body. Nine times out of ten a needless and awkward expression, meaning no more than the simple word *students.*

A member of the student body	A student
Popular with the student body	Liked by the students

Thanking you in advance. This sounds as if the writer meant, "It will not be worth my while to write to you again." In making your request, write, "Will you please," or "I shall be obliged." Then later, if you feel moved to do so, or if the circumstances call for it, write a letter of acknowledgment.

That, which. *That* is the defining or restrictive pronoun, *which* the non-defining or nonrestrictive. See under Rule 3.

The lawn mower that is broken is in the garage. (Tells which one.)

The lawn mower, which is broken, is in the garage. (Adds a fact about the only mower in question.)

The use of *which* for *that* is common in written and spoken language ("Let us now go even unto Bethlehem, and see this thing which is come to pass.") Occasionally *which* seems preferable to *that* as in the sentence from the Bible. But it would be a convenience to all if these two pronouns were used with precision. The careful writer, watchful for small conveniences, goes which-hunting, removes the defining *whiches*, and by so doing improves his work.

The foreseeable future. A cliché and a fuzzy one. How much of the future is foreseeable? Ten minutes? Ten years? Any of it? By whom is it foreseeable? Seers? Experts? Everybody?

They. Not to be used when the antecedent is a distributive expression such as *each, each one, everybody, every one, many a man.* Use the singular pronoun.

Every one of us knows they are fallible.	Every one of us knows he is fallible.
Everyone in the community, whether they are a member of the Association or not, is invited to attend.	Everyone in the community, whether he is a member of the Association or not, is invited to attend.

Similar to this, but with even less justification, is the use of the plural pronoun with the antecedent *anybody, any one, somebody, some one,* the intention being either to avoid the awkward "he or she," or to avoid committing oneself to either. Some bashful speakers even say, "A friend of mine told me that they, etc."

Use *he* with all such words, unless the antecedent is or must be feminine.

Tortuous, torturous. A winding road is *tortuous,* a painful ordeal is *torturous.* Both words carry the idea of "twist," the twist having been a form of torture.

Transpire. Not to be used in the sense of *happen, come to pass.* Many writers so use it (usually when groping toward imagined elegance), but their usage finds little support in the Latin "breathe across or through." Correct, however, in the sense of *become known.* "Eventually, the grim account of his villainy transpired." (Literally, leaked through or out.)

Type. Not a synonym for *kind of.* The examples below are common vulgarisms.

That type employee	That kind of employee
I dislike that type notoriety.	I dislike that kind of notoriety (notoriety of that sort).
Her type beauty	Her kind of beauty
A new type plane	A plane of a new design (new kind)

Unique. Means *being without a like or equal.* Hence, there can be no degrees of uniqueness.

It was the most unique egg beater on the market.	It was a unique egg beater.
The balancing act was very unique.	The balancing act was unique.
Of all the spiders, the one that lives in a bubble under water is the most unique.	Among spiders, the one that lives in a bubble under water is unique.

Very. Use this word sparingly. Where emphasis is necessary, use words strong in themselves.

While. Avoid the indiscriminate use of this word for *and, but,* and *although.* Many writers use it frequently as a sub-

48

stitute for *and* or *but,* either from a mere desire to vary the connective, or because they are not sure which of the two connectives is the more appropriate. In this use it is best replaced by a semicolon.

The office and salesrooms are on the ground floor, while the rest of the building is devoted to manufacturing.	The office and salesrooms are on the ground floor; the rest of the building is devoted to manufacturing.

Its use as a virtual equivalent of *although* is allowable in sentences where this leads to no ambiguity or absurdity.

While I admire his energy, I wish it were employed in a better cause.

This is entirely correct, as shown by the paraphrase,

I admire his energy; at the same time I wish it were employed in a better cause.

Compare:

While the temperature reaches 90 or 95 degrees in the daytime, the nights are often chilly.	Although the temperature reaches 90 or 95 degrees in the daytime, the nights are often chilly.

The paraphrase,

The temperature reaches 90 or 95 degrees in the daytime; at the same time the nights are often chilly,

shows why the use of *while* is incorrect.

In general, the writer will do well to use *while* only with strict literalness, in the sense of *during the time that.*

Whom. Often incorrectly used for *who* before *he said* or similar expressions, when it is really the subject of a following verb.

His brother, whom he said would send him the money	His brother, who he said would send him the money

-wise. Not to be used indiscriminately as a pseudosuffix: *taxwise, pricewise, marriagewise, prosewise, saltwater taffy-wise.* Chiefly useful when it means *in the manner of: clockwise.* There is not a noun in the language to which *-wise* cannot be added if the spirit moves one to do so. The sober writer will abstain from the use of this wild syllable.

Worth while. Overworked as a term of vague approval and (with *not*) of disapproval. Strictly applicable only to actions: "Is it worth while to telegraph?"

His books are not worth while.	His books are not worth reading (are not worth one's while to read; do not repay reading).

Would. A conditional statement in the first person requires *should,* not *would.*

I should not have succeeded without his help.

The equivalent of *shall* in indirect quotation after a verb in the past tense is *should,* not *would.*

He predicted that before long we should have a great surprise.

Would is commonly used to express habitual or repeated action. ("He would get up early and prepare his own breakfast before he went to work.") But when the idea of habit or repetition is expressed, in such phrases as *once a year, every day, each Sunday,* the past tense, without *would,* is usually sufficient, and from its brevity, more emphatic.

Once a year he would visit the old mansion.	Once a year he visited the old mansion.

In narrative writing, always indicate the transition from the general to the particular, that is, from sentences that merely state a general habit to those that express the action of a specific day or period. Failure to indicate the change will cause confusion.

Townsend would get up early and prepare his own breakfast. If the day was cold, he filled the stove and had a warm fire burning before he left the house. On his way out to the garage, he noticed that there were footprints in the new-fallen snow on the porch.

The reader is lost, having received no signal that Townsend has changed from a mere man of habit to a man who has seen a particular thing on a particular day.

Townsend would get up early and prepare his own breakfast. If the day was cold, he filled the stove and had a warm fire burning before he left the house. One morning in January, on his way out to the garage, he noticed that there were footprints in the new-fallen snow on the porch.

V

An Approach to Style

(With a List of Reminders)

Up to this point, the book has been concerned with what is correct, or acceptable, in the use of English. In this final chapter, we approach style in its broader meaning: style in the sense of what is distinguished and distinguishing. Here we leave solid ground. Who can confidently say what ignites a certain combination of words, causing them to explode in the mind? Who knows why certain notes in music are capable of stirring the listener deeply, though the same notes, slightly rearranged, are impotent? These are high mysteries, and this chapter is a mystery story, thinly disguised. There is no satisfactory explanation of style, no infallible guide to good writing, no assurance that a person who thinks clearly will be able to write clearly, no key that unlocks the door, no inflexible rule by which the young writer may shape his course. He will often find himself steering by stars that are disturbingly in motion.

The preceding chapters contain instructions drawn from established English usage; this one contains advice drawn from a writer's experience of writing. Since the book is a rulebook, these cautionary remarks, these subtly dangerous hints, are presented in the form of rules, but they are, in essence, mere gentle reminders: they state what most of us know and, at times, forget.

Style is an increment in writing. When we speak of Fitzgerald's style, we don't mean his command of the relative pronoun, we mean the sound his words make on paper. Every writer, by the way he uses the language, reveals something of his spirit, his habits, his capacities, his bias. This is inevitable, as well as enjoyable. All writing is communication; creative writing is communication through revelation— it is the Self escaping into the open. No writer long remains incognito.

If the student doubts that style is something of a mystery, let him try rewriting a familiar sentence and see what happens. Any much-quoted sentence will do. Suppose we take "These are the times that try men's souls." Here we have eight short, easy words, forming a simple declarative sentence. The sentence contains no flashy ingredient, such as "Damn the torpedoes!" and the words, as you see, are ordinary. Yet in that arrangement they have shown great durability; the sentence is well along in its second century. Now compose a few variations:

> Times like these try men's souls.
> How trying it is to live in these times!
> These are trying times for men's souls.
> Soulwise, these are trying times.

It seems unlikely that Thomas Paine could have made his sentiment stick if he had couched it in any of these forms. But why not? No fault of grammar can be detected in them, and in every case the meaning is clear. Each version is correct, and each, for some reason that we can't readily put our finger on, is marked for oblivion. We could, of course, talk about "rhythm" and "cadence," but the talk would be vague and unconvincing. We could declare "soulwise" to be a silly word, inappropriate to the occasion; but even that won't do—it does not answer the main question. Are we even sure "soulwise" is silly? If "otherwise" is a serviceable word, what's the matter with "soulwise?"

Here is another sentence, this one by a later Tom. It is not a famous sentence, although its author (Thomas Wolfe) is well known. "Quick are the mouths of earth, and quick the teeth that fed upon this loveliness." The sentence would not take a prize for clarity, and rhetorically it is at the opposite pole from "These are the times." Try it in a different form, without the inversions:

> The mouths of earth are quick, and the teeth
> that fed upon this loveliness are quick, too.

The author's meaning is still intact, but not his overpowering emotion. What was poetical and sensuous has become prosy and wooden; instead of the secret sounds of beauty, we are left with the simple crunch of mastication. (Whether Mr. Wolfe was guilty of overwriting is, of course, another question—one that is not pertinent here.)

With some writers, style not only reveals the spirit of the man, it reveals his identity, as surely as would his fingerprints. Here, following, are two brief passages from the works of two American novelists. The subject in each case is languor. In both, the words used are ordinary, and there is nothing eccentric about the construction.

He did not still feel weak, he was merely luxuriating in that supremely gutful lassitude of convalescence in which time, hurry, doing, did not exist, the accumulating seconds and minutes and hours to which in its well state the body is slave both waking and sleeping, now reversed and time now the lip-server and mendicant to the body's pleasure instead of the body thrall to time's headlong course.

Manuel drank his brandy. He felt sleepy himself. It was too hot to go out into the town. Besides there was nothing to do. He wanted to see Zurito. He would go to sleep while he waited.

54

Anyone acquainted with Faulkner and Hemingway will have recognized them in these passages and perceived which was which. How different are their languors!

Or take two American poets, stopping at evening. One stops by woods, the other by laughing flesh.

> My little horse must think it queer
> To stop without a farmhouse near
> Between the woods and frozen lake
> The darkest evening of the year.[1]

> I have perceived that to be with those I like is enough,
> To stop in company with the rest at evening is enough,
> To be surrounded by beautiful, curious, breathing,
>   laughing flesh is enough . . .

Because of the characteristic styles, there is little question of identity here, and if the situations were reversed, with Whitman stopping by woods and Frost by laughing flesh (not one of his regularly scheduled stops), the reader would still know who was who.

Young writers often suppose that style is a garnish for the meat of prose, a sauce by which a dull dish is made palatable. Style has no such separate entity; it is non-detachable, unfilterable. The beginner should approach style warily, realizing that it is himself he is approaching, no other; and he should begin by turning resolutely away from all devices that are popularly believed to indicate style—all mannerisms, tricks, adornments. The approach to style is by way of plainness, simplicity, orderliness, sincerity.

Writing is, for most, laborious and slow. The mind travels faster than the pen; consequently, writing becomes a question of learning to make occasional wing shots, bringing down the bird of thought as it flashes by. A writer is a gunner, sometimes waiting in his blind for something to come in, sometimes roaming the countryside hoping to

[1] Excerpt from "Stopping by Woods on a Snowy Evening" in *Complete Poems of Robert Frost*. Copyright 1930, 1949, by Henry Holt and Company, Inc. By permission of the publishers.

scare something up. Like other gunners, he must cultivate patience: he may have to work many covers to bring down one partridge. Here, following, are some suggestions and cautionary hints that may help the beginner find his way to a satisfactory style.

1. Place yourself in the background.

Write in a way* that draws the reader's attention to the sense and substance of the writing, rather than to the mood and temper of the author. If the writing is solid and good, the mood and temper of the writer will become revealed finally, and not at the expense of the work. Therefore, the first piece of advice is this: to achieve style, begin by affecting none—that is, place yourself in the background. A careful and honest writer does not need to worry about style. As he becomes proficient in the use of the language, his style will emerge, because he himself will emerge, and when this happens he will find it increasingly easy to break through the barriers that separate him from other minds, other hearts—which is, of course, the purpose of writing, as well as its principal reward. Fortunately, the act of composition, or creation, disciplines the mind; writing is one way to go about thinking, and the practice and habit of writing not only drain the mind but supply it, too.

2. Write in a way that comes naturally.

Write in a way that comes easily and naturally to you, using words and phrases that come readily to hand. But do not assume that because you have acted naturally your product is without flaw.

The use of language begins with imitation. The infant imitates the sounds made by its parents; the child imitates first the spoken language, then the stuff of books. The imitative life continues long after the writer is on his own in the language, for it is almost impossible to avoid imitating what one admires. Never imitate consciously, but do not worry about being an imitator; take pains instead to admire what is good. Then when you write in a way that comes naturally, you will echo the halloos that bear repeating.

3. Work from a suitable design.

Before beginning to compose something, gauge the nature and extent of the enterprise and work from a suitable design. (See under Chapter II, Rule 8.) Design informs even the simplest structure, whether of brick-and-steel or of prose. You raise a pup tent from one sort of vision, a cathedral from another. This does not mean that you must sit with a blueprint always in front of you, merely that you had best anticipate what you are getting into. To compose a laundry list, a writer can work directly from the pile of soiled garments, ticking them off one by one. But to write a biography, the writer will need at least a rough scheme; he cannot plunge in blindly and start ticking off fact after fact about his man, lest he miss the forest for the trees and there be no end to his labors.

Sometimes, of course, impulse and emotion are more compelling than design. A deeply troubled person, composing a letter appealing for mercy or for love, had best not attempt to organize his emotions; his prose will have a better chance if he leaves his emotions in disarray, which he'll probably have to do anyway, since one's feelings do not usually lend themselves to rearrangement. But even the kind of writing that is essentially adventurous and impetuous will on examination be found to have a secret plan: Columbus didn't just sail, he sailed west, and the new world took shape from this simple, and we now think sensible, design.

4. Write with nouns and verbs.

Write with nouns and verbs, not with adjectives and adverbs. The adjective hasn't been built that can pull a weak or inaccurate noun out of a tight place. This is not to disparage adjectives and adverbs; they are indispensable parts of speech. Occasionally they surprise us with their power, as in

> Up the airy mountain,
>   Down the rushy glen,
> We daren't go a-hunting
>   For fear of little men . . .

The nouns *mountain* and *glen* are accurate enough, but had the mountain not become airy, the glen rushy, William Allingham might never have got off the ground with his poem. In general, however, it is nouns and verbs, not their assistants, that give to good writing its toughness and color.

5. *Revise and rewrite.*

Revising is part of writing. Few writers are so expert that they can produce what they are after on the first try. Quite often the writer will discover, on examining the completed work, that there are serious flaws in the arrangement of the material, calling for transpositions. When this is the case, he can save himself much labor and time by using scissors on his manuscript, cutting it to pieces and fitting the pieces together in a better order. If the work merely needs shortening, a pencil is the most useful tool; but if it needs rearranging, or stirring up, scissors should be brought into play. Do not be afraid to seize whatever you have written and cut it to ribbons; it can always be restored to its original condition in the morning, if that course seems best. Remember, it is no sign of weakness or defeat that your manuscript ends up in need of major surgery. This is a common occurrence in all writing, and among the best writers.

6. *Do not overwrite.*

Rich, ornate prose is hard to digest, generally unwholesome, and sometimes nauseating. If the sickly sweet word, the overblown phrase, are a writer's natural form of expression, as is sometimes the case, he will have to compensate for it by a show of vigor, and by writing something as meritorious as the Song of Songs, which is Solomon's.

7. *Do not overstate.*

When you overstate, the reader will be instantly on guard, and everything that has preceded your overstatement, as well as everything that follows it, will be suspect in his mind because he has lost confidence in your judgment or your poise. Overstatement is one of the common faults. A single overstatement, wherever or however it occurs, diminishes the whole, and a single carefree superlative has the power to destroy, for the reader, the object of the writer's enthusiasm.

8. *Avoid the use of qualifiers.*

Rather, very, little, pretty—these are the leeches that infest the pond of prose, sucking the blood of words. The constant use of the adjective *little* (except to indicate size) is particularly depleting; we should all try to do a little better, we should all be very watchful of this rule, for it is a rather important one and we are pretty sure to violate it now and then.

9. *Do not affect a breezy manner.*

The volume of writing is enormous, these days, and much of it has a sort of windiness about it, almost as though the author were in a state of euphoria. "Spontaneous me," sang Whitman, and in his innocence let loose the hordes of uninspired scribblers who would one day confuse spontaneity with genius.

The breezy style is often the work of an egocentric, the person who imagines that everything that pops into his head is of general interest and that uninhibited prose creates high spirits and carries the day. Open any alumni magazine, turn to the class notes, and you are quite likely to encounter old Spontaneous Me at work—an introductory paragraph that goes something like this:

Well, chums, here I am again with my bagful of dirt about your disorderly classmates, after spending a helluva weekend in

59

N'Yawk trying to view the Columbia game from behind two bumbershoots and a glazed cornea. And speaking of news, howzabout tossing a few chirce nuggets my way?

This is an extreme example, but the same wind blows, at lesser velocities, across vast expanses of journalistic prose. The author in this case has managed in two sentences to commit most of the unpardonable sins: he obviously has nothing to say, he is showing off and directing the attention of the reader to himself, he is using slang with neither provocation nor ingenuity, he adopts a patronizing air by throwing in the word "chirce," he is tasteless, humorless (though full of fun), dull, and empty. He has not done his work. Compare his opening remarks with the following—a plunge directly into the news:

Clyde Crawford, who stroked the varsity shell in 1928, is swinging an oar again after a lapse of thirty years. Clyde resigned last spring as executive sales manager of the Indiana Flotex Company and is now a gondolier in Venice.

This, although conventional, is compact, informative, unpretentious. The writer has dug up an item of news and presented it in a straightforward manner. What the first writer tried to accomplish by cutting rhetorical capers and by breeziness, the second writer managed to achieve by good reporting, by keeping a tight rein on his material, and by staying out of the act.

10. Use orthodox spelling.

In ordinary composition, use orthodox spelling. Do not write *nite* for *night*, *thru* for *through*, *pleez* for *please*, unless you plan to introduce a complete system of simplified spelling and are prepared to take the consequences.

In the original edition of *The Elements of Style*, there was a chapter on spelling. In it, the author had this to say:

The spelling of English words is not fixed and invariable, nor does it depend on any other authority than general agreement. At the present day there is practically unanimous agreement as to the spelling of most words. . . . At any given moment, however, a relatively small number of words may be spelled in more than one way. Gradually, as a rule, one of these forms comes to be generally preferred, and the less customary form comes to look obsolete and is discarded. From time to time new forms, mostly simplifications, are introduced by innovators, and either win their place or die of neglect.

The practical objection to unaccepted and over-simplified spellings is the disfavor with which they are received by the reader. They distract his attention and exhaust his patience. He reads the form *though* automatically, without thought of its needless complexity; he reads the abbreviation *tho* and mentally supplies the missing letters, at the cost of a fraction of his attention. The writer has defeated his own purpose.

The language manages somehow to keep pace with events. A word that has taken hold recently is *thruway;* it was born of necessity and is apparently here to stay. In combination with "way," "thru" is more serviceable than "through"; it is a high-speed word for readers who are going seventy. *Throughway* would be too long to fit on a roadsign, too slow to serve the speeding eye. It is conceivable that because of our thruways, *through* will eventually become *thru*—after many more thousands of miles of travel.

11. Do not explain too much.

It is seldom advisable to tell all. Be sparing, for instance, in the use of adverbs after "he said," "she replied," and the like. (*he said consolingly; she replied grumblingly.*) Let the conversation itself disclose the speaker's manner or condition. Dialogue heavily weighted with adverbs after the attributive verb is cluttery and annoying. Inexperienced writers not only overwork their adverbs, they load their attributives with explanatory verbs, sometimes even with transitive verbs used intransitively: *he consoled, she congratulated.* They do this, apparently, in the belief that the word "said" is always in need of support, or because they have been told to do it by experts in the art of bad writing.

12. *Do not construct awkward adverbs.*

Adverbs are easy to build. Take an adjective or a participle, add *ly,* and behold! you have an adverb. But you'd probably be better off without it. Do not write *tangledly.* The word itself is just a tangle. Do not even write *tiredly.* Nobody says *tangledly* and not many people say *tiredly.* Words that are not used orally are seldom the ones to put on paper.

He climbed tiredly to bed.   He climbed wearily to bed.
The lamp cord lay tangledly   The lamp cord lay in tan-
beneath his chair.   gles beneath his chair.

Do not dress words up by adding *ly* to them, as though putting a hat on a horse.

overly   over
firstly   first
muchly   much

13. *Make sure the reader knows who is speaking.*

Dialogue is a total loss unless you indicate who the speaker is. In long dialogue passages containing no attributives, the reader may become lost and be compelled to go back and reread in order to puzzle the thing out. This is an imposition on the reader, to say nothing of the damage to the work.

In dialogue, make sure that your attributives do not awkwardly interrupt a spoken sentence. Place them where the break would come naturally in speech—that is, where the speaker would pause for emphasis, or take a breath. The best test for locating an attributive is to speak the sentence aloud.

"Now, my boy, we shall   "Now, my boy," he said,
see," he said, "how well you   "we shall see how well you
have learned your lesson."   have learned your lesson."

"What's more, they would   "What's more," he added,
never," he added, "consent to   "they would never consent to
the plan."   the plan."

14. Avoid fancy words.

Avoid the elaborate, the pretentious, the coy, and the cute. Do not be tempted by a twenty-dollar word when there is a ten-center handy, ready and able. Anglo-Saxon is a livelier tongue than Latin, so use Anglo-Saxon words; in this, as in so many matters pertaining to style, one's ear must be one's guide: *gut* is a lustier noun than *intestine,* but the two words are not interchangeable, because *gut* is often inappropriate, being too coarse for the context. Never call a stomach a tummy without good reason.

If you admire fancy words, if every sky is *beauteous,* every blonde *curvaceous,* if you are tickled by *discombobulate,* you will have a bad time with Reminder 14. What is wrong, you ask, with *beauteous?* No one knows, for sure. There is nothing wrong, really, with any word—all are good, but some are better than others. A matter of ear, a matter of reading the books that sharpen the ear.

The line between the fancy and the plain, between the atrocious and the felicitous, is sometimes alarmingly fine. The opening phrase of the Gettysburg address is close to the line, at least by our standards today, and Mr. Lincoln, knowingly or unknowingly, was flirting with disaster when he wrote "Four score and seven years ago." The President could have got into his sentence with plain "Eighty-seven," a saving of two words and less of a strain on the listeners' powers of multiplication. But Lincoln's ear must have told him to go ahead with four score and seven. By doing so, he achieved cadence while skirting the edge of fanciness. Suppose he had blundered over the line and written, "In the year of our Lord seventeen hundred and seventy-six." His speech would have sustained a heavy blow. Or suppose he had settled for "Eighty-seven." In that case he would have got into his introductory sentence too quickly; the timing would have been bad.

The question of "ear" is vital. Only the writer whose ear is reliable is in a position to use bad grammar deliberately; only he knows for sure when a colloquialism is better than formal phrasing; only he is able to sustain his work at the level of good taste. So cock your ear. Years ago, students were warned not to end a sentence with a preposition; time, of course, has softened that rigid decree. Not only is the preposition acceptable at the end, sometimes it is more effective in that spot than anywhere else. "A claw hammer, not an ax, was the tool he murdered her with." This is preferable to, "A claw hammer, not an ax, was the tool with which he murdered her." Why? Because it sounds more violent, more like murder. A matter of ear.

And would you write, "The worst tennis player around here is I," or, "The worst tennis player around here is me"? The first is good grammar, the second is good judgment—although the *me* might not do in all contexts.

The split infinitive is another trick of rhetoric in which the ear must be quicker than the handbook. Some infinitives seem to improve on being split, just as a stick of round stove-wood does. "I cannot bring myself to really like the fellow." The sentence is relaxed, the meaning is clear, the violation is harmless and scarcely perceptible. Put the other way, the sentence becomes stiff, needlessly formal. A matter of ear.

There are times when the ear not only guides a man through difficult situations but also saves him from minor or major embarrassments of prose. The ear, for example, must decide when to omit *that* from a sentence, when to retain it. "He knew he could do it" is preferable to "He knew that he could do it"—simpler and just as clear. But in many cases, the *that* is needed. "He felt that his big nose, which was sunburned, made him look ridiculous." Omit the *that* and you have, "He felt his big nose . . ."

15. Do not use dialect unless your ear is good.

Do not attempt to use dialect unless you are a devoted student of the tongue you hope to reproduce. If you use dialect, be consistent. The reader will become impatient or confused if he finds two or more versions of the same word or expression. In dialect it is necessary to spell phonetically,

64

or at least ingeniously, to capture unusual inflections. Take, for example, the word *once*; it often appears in dialect writing as *oncet*, but *oncet* looks as though it should be pronounced "onset." A better spelling would be *wunst*. But if you write it *oncet* once, write it that way throughout. The best dialect writers, by and large, are economical of their talents: they use the minimum, not the maximum, of deviation from the norm, thus sparing the reader as well as convincing him.

16. Be clear.

Clarity is not the prize in writing, nor is it always the principal mark of a good style. There are occasions when obscurity serves a literary yearning, if not a literary purpose, and there are writers whose mien is more overcast than clear. But since writing is communication, clarity can only be a virtue. And although there is no substitute for merit in writing, clarity comes closest to being one. Even to a writer who is being intentionally obscure or wild of tongue we can say, "Be obscure clearly! Be wild of tongue in a way we can understand!" Even to writers of market letters, telling us (but not telling us) which securities are promising, we can say, "Be cagey plainly! Be elliptical in a straightforward fashion!"

Clarity, clarity, clarity. When you become hopelessly mired in a sentence, it is best to start fresh; do not try to fight your way through against the terrible odds of syntax. Usually what is wrong is that the construction has become too involved at some point; the sentence needs to be broken apart and replaced by two or more shorter sentences.

Muddiness is not merely a disturber of prose, it is a destroyer of life, of hope: death on the highway caused by a badly worded roadsign, heartbreak among lovers caused by a misplaced phrase in a well-intentioned letter, anguish of a traveler expecting to be met at a railroad station and not being met because of a slipshod telegram. Usually we think only of the ludicrous aspect of ambiguity; we enjoy it when the *Times* tells us that Nelson Rockefeller is "chairman of the Museum of Modern Art, which he entered in a fireman's raincoat during a recent fire, and founded the Museum of Primitive Art." This we all love. But think of the tragedies that are rooted in ambiguity; think of that side, and be clear! When you say something, make sure you have said it. The chances of your having said it are only fair.

17. Do not inject opinion.

Unless there is a good reason for its being there, do not inject opinion into a piece of writing. We all have opinions about almost everything, and the temptation to toss them in is great. To air one's views gratuitously, however, is to imply that the demand for them is brisk, which may not be the case, and which, in any event, may not be relevant. Opinions scattered indiscriminately about leave the mark of egotism on a work. Similarly, to air one's views at an improper time may be in bad taste. If you have received a letter inviting you to speak at the dedication of a new cat hospital, and you hate cats, your reply, declining the invitation, does not necessarily have to cover the full range of your emotions. You must make it clear that you will not attend, but you do not have to let fly at cats. The writer of the letter asked a civil question; attack cats, then, only if you can do so with good humor, good taste, and in such a way that your answer will be courteous as well as responsive. Since you are out of sympathy with cats, you may quite properly give this as a reason for not appearing at the dedicatory ceremonies of a cat hospital. But bear in mind that your opinion of cats was not sought, only your services as a speaker. Try to keep things straight.

18. Use figures of speech sparingly.

The simile is a common device and a useful one, but similes coming in rapid fire, one right on top of another, are more distracting than illuminating. The reader needs time to catch his breath; he can't be expected to compare every-thing with something else, and no relief in sight.

When you use metaphor, do not mix it up. That is, don't start by calling something a swordfish and end by calling it an hourglass.

19. Do not take shortcuts at the cost of clarity.

Do not use initials for the names of organizations or movements unless you are certain the initials will be readily understood. Write things out. Not everyone knows that N.A.A.C.P. means National Association for the Advance-ment of Colored People, and even if everyone did, there are babies being born every minute who will some day en-counter the name for the first time. They deserve to see the words, not simply the initials. A good rule is to start your article by writing out names in full, and then later, when the reader has got his bearings, shorten them.

Many shortcuts are self-defeating; they waste the reader's time instead of conserving it. There are all sorts of rhetorical gambits and devices that attract writers who hope to be pithy, but most of them are simply bothersome. The longest way round is usually the shortest way home, and the one truly reliable shortcut in writing is to choose words that are strong and sure-footed, to carry the reader on his way.

20. Avoid foreign languages.

The writer will often find it convenient or necessary to borrow from other languages. Some writers, however, from sheer exuberance or a desire to show off, sprinkle their work liberally with foreign expressions, with no regard for the reader's comfort. It is a bad habit. Write in English.

21. Prefer the standard to the offbeat.

The young writer will be drawn at every turn toward eccentricities in language. He will hear the beat of new vocabularies, the exciting rhythms of special segments of his society, each speaking a language of its own. All of us come under the spell of these unsettling drums; the problem, for the beginner, is to listen to them, learn the words, feel the excitement, and not be carried away.

Today, the language of advertising enjoys an enormous circulation. With its deliberate infractions of grammatical rules and its crossbreeding of the parts of speech, it profoundly influences the tongues and pens of children and adults. Your new kitchen range is so revolutionary it *obsoletes* all other ranges. Your counter top is beautiful because it is *accessorized* with gold-plated faucets. Your cigarette tastes good *like* a cigarette should. And *like the man says,* you will want to try one. You will also, in all probability, want to try writing that way, using that language. You do so at your peril, for it is the language of mutilation.

Advertisers are quite understandably interested in what they call "attention getting." The man photographed must have lost an eye or grown a pink beard, or he must have three arms or be sitting wrong end to on a horse. This technique is proper in its place, which is the world of selling, but the young writer had best not adopt the device of mutilation in ordinary composition, whose purpose is to engage, not paralyze, the reader's senses. Our advice is to buy the gold-plated faucets if you will, but do not accessorize your prose. To use the language well, do not begin by hacking it to bits; accept the whole body of it, cherish its classic form, its variety, and its richness.

Another segment of society that has constructed a language of its own is business. The businessman says that ink erasers are *in short supply,* that he has *updated* the next shipment of these erasers, and that he will *finalize* his recommendations at the next meeting of the board. He is speaking a language that is familiar to him and dear to him. Its portentous nouns and verbs invest ordinary events with high adventure; the executive walks among ink erasers caparisoned like a knight. This we should be tolerant of—every man of spirit wants to ride a white horse. The only question

68

is whether his vocabulary is helpful to ordinary prose. Usually, the same ideas can be expressed less formidably, if one wishes to do so. A good many of the special words of business seem designed more to express the user's dreams than his precise meaning. Not all such words, of course, can be dismissed summarily—indeed, no word in the language can be dismissed offhand by anyone who has a healthy curiosity. *Update* isn't a bad word; in the right setting it is useful. In the wrong setting, though, it is destructive, and the trouble with adopting coinages too quickly is that they will bedevil one by insinuating themselves where they do not belong. This may sound like rhetorical snobbery, or plain stuffiness; but the writer will discover, in the course of his work, that the setting of a word is just as restrictive as the setting of a jewel. The general rule, here, is to prefer the standard. *Finalize,* for instance, is not standard: it is special, and it is a peculiarly fuzzy and silly word. Does it mean *terminate,* or does it mean *put into final form?* One can't be sure, really, what it means, and one gets the impression that the person using it doesn't know either, and doesn't want to know.

The special vocabularies of the law, of the military, of government, are familiar to most of us. Even the world of criticism has a modest pouch of private words (*luminous, taut*), whose only virtue is that they are exceptionally nimble and can escape from the garden of meaning over the wall. Of these Critical words, Wolcott Gibbs once wrote: ". . . they are detached from the language and inflated like little balloons." The young writer should learn to spot them—words that at first glance seem freighted with delicious meaning but that soon burst in air, leaving nothing but a memory of bright sound.

The language is perpetually in flux: it is a living stream, shifting, changing, receiving new strength from a thousand tributaries, losing old forms in the backwaters of time. To suggest that a young writer not swim in the main stream of this turbulence would be foolish indeed, and such is not the intent of these cautionary remarks. The intent is to suggest that in choosing between the formal and the informal, the regular and the offbeat, the general and the special, the orthodox and the heretical, the beginner err on the side of conservatism, on the side of established usage. No idiom is taboo, no accent forbidden; there simply is a better chance of doing well if the writer holds a steady course, enters the stream of English quietly, and does not thrash about.

"But," the student may ask, "what if it comes natural to me to experiment rather than conform? What if I am a pioneer, or even a genius?" Answer: then be one. But do not forget that what may seem like pioneering may be merely evasion, or laziness—the disinclination to submit to discipline. Writing good standard English is no cinch, and before you have managed it you will have encountered enough rough country to satisfy even the most adventurous spirit.

Style takes its final shape more from attitudes of mind than from principles of composition, for as an elderly practitioner once remarked, "Writing is an act of faith, not a trick of grammar." This moral observation would have no place in a rulebook were it not that style *is* the writer, and therefore what a man is, rather than what he knows, will at last determine his style. If one is to write, one must believe—in the truth and worth of the scrawl, in the ability of the reader to receive and decode the message. No one can write decently who is distrustful of the reader's intelligence, or whose attitude is patronizing.

Many references have been made in this book to "the reader"—he has been much in the news. It is now necessary to warn the writer that his concern for the reader must be pure: he must sympathize with the reader's plight (most readers are in trouble about half the time) but never seek to know his wants. The whole duty of a writer is to please and satisfy himself, and the true writer always plays to an audience of one. Let him start sniffing the air, or glancing at the Trend Machine, and he is as good as dead, although he may make a nice living.

Full of his beliefs, sustained and elevated by the power of his purpose, armed with the rules of grammar, the writer is ready for exposure. At this point, he may well pattern himself on the fully exposed cow of Robert Louis Stevenson's rhyme. This friendly and commendable animal, you may recall, was "blown by all the winds that pass/And wet with all the showers." And so must the young writer be. In our modern idiom, we would say that he must get wet all over. Mr. Stevenson, working in a plainer style, said it with felicity, and suddenly one cow, out of so many, received the gift of immortality. Like the steadfast writer, she is at home in the wind and the rain; and thanks to one moment of felicity, she will live on and on and on.